Spirit Empowered:

Living a Life of Grace, Compassion, and Forgiveness

All rights reserved.

No parts of this book may be reproduced, distributed, or transmitted in any form or by any means, including photocopying, recording, or other electronic or mechanical methods, without the publisher's prior written permission.

This Book is Dedicated To...

This book is dedicated to those seeking a deeper, more authentic Christian life who long to break free from negativity and embrace the transformative power of the Holy Spirit. It is for those ready to cultivate grace, compassion, and forgiveness in their own lives and relationships and who desire to be empowered by the Spirit to impact the world around them positively.

A Survey of Determination: Why Read This Book?

In a world often filled with anger, bitterness, and division, "Spirit Empowered" offers a refreshing and much-needed message of hope and healing. This book explores the profound impact of the Holy Spirit on our lives, guiding readers towards a life characterized by:

Inner Transformation: Discover how the Holy Spirit empowers us to overcome negativity, release bitterness, and embrace genuine forgiveness.

Spiritual Growth: Learn how to cultivate a Spirit-filled heart, deepen your relationship with God, and experience His guidance in daily life.

Relational Healing: Gain practical tools to mend broken relationships, foster unity within communities, and build a culture of compassion.

Empowered Living: Uncover the secrets to walking in the Spirit's power, experiencing true freedom, and becoming a vessel of God's love to the world.

"Spirit Empowered" is more than just a book; it invites a transformation journey. Through insightful teaching, practical exercises, and inspiring stories, you'll be equipped to:

Understand the role of the Holy Spirit: Gain a deeper understanding of who the Holy Spirit is and how He works in our lives.

Overcome negativity: Learn how to identify and release bitterness, anger, and malice, replacing them with kindness and compassion.

Embrace forgiveness: Discover the true meaning of biblical forgiveness and learn how to extend it to others, even in challenging situations.

Live in harmony: Explore how the Holy Spirit fosters unity and empowers us to build strong, compassionate communities.

Walk in daily empowerment: Develop spiritual disciplines that help you stay connected to the Spirit and live a life filled with grace and purpose.

If you're ready to experience the transformative power of the Holy Spirit and live a life that genuinely reflects Christ's love, then this book is for you.

Contents

Contents 6

Introduction: Embracing a Spirit-Empowered Life 8

Chapter 1: The Holy Spirit – Our Source of Empowerment 10

Chapter 2: Not Grieving the Holy Spirit – Maintaining a Spirit-Filled Heart 16

Chapter 3: Letting Go – Releasing Bitterness, Anger, and Malice 23

Chapter 4: Embracing Grace – Cultivating Kindness and Compassion 32

Chapter 5: The Art of Forgiveness – Reflecting Christ's Forgiveness 39

Chapter 6: Living in Harmony – Building Unified Communities 47

Chapter 7: Daily Empowerment – Walking in the Spirit 55

Conclusion: A Spirit-Empowered Journey of Transformation 62

30-Day Challenge: Intentionally Listening to the Spirit 69

Halfway Through 85

Appendices 102

Dear Reader,

Before you embark on this journey of discovering the Spirit-empowered life, I want you to know this: you are not alone.

As you delve into these pages, you might encounter truths that challenge you, stir up deep emotions, or even expose areas where you've struggled. You might feel overwhelmed by the prospect of change or discouraged by past failures. In those moments, remember that God sees you, understands you, and is with you every step of the way.

The Christian life is not a solo endeavor. It's a journey we walk hand-in-hand with the Holy Spirit, our constant companion, comforter, and guide. He empowers us to overcome challenges, break free from old patterns, and step into the fullness of life that God intends for us.

So, don't give up. Don't let discouragement or the weight of past mistakes hold you back. Embrace God's grace so freely, and allow the Holy Spirit to lead you into a life of greater freedom, purpose, and joy.

Throughout these pages, you'll find practical tools, inspiring stories, and biblical truths to equip you on this journey. But most importantly, you'll encounter the transformative power of the Holy Spirit, who is ready to work in and through you in extraordinary ways.

With you on the journey,

Your Sister In Christ

Introduction:
Embracing a Spirit-Empowered Life

In a world that often pulls us towards selfishness, negativity, and division, it's easy to become trapped in cycles of hurt, bitterness, and unforgiveness. We long for transformation – in our hearts, relationships, and the world – but our strength often fails. The truth is lasting change, the kind that genuinely reflects Christ's love, is simply not possible on our own. Our natural inclinations, our "flesh," as the Bible calls it, gravitate towards self-preservation and self-interest. We need a power greater than ourselves to break these chains and set us on a new path.

That's where the Holy Spirit comes in.

This book, "Spirit Empowered: Living a Life of Grace, Compassion, and Forgiveness," invites you to discover the incredible transforming power of the Holy Spirit. It explores what it means to live a Spirit-empowered life characterized by the very qualities we often struggle to embody: grace, compassion, and forgiveness. We'll delve into the profound truth of Ephesians 4:30-32, where Paul urges us to "be kind and compassionate to one another, forgiving each other, just as in Christ God forgave you." But we'll go beyond simply understanding these words; we'll discover how the Holy Spirit empowers us to live them out.

This book is your guide to harnessing the Spirit's power to overcome negativity, cultivate genuine forgiveness, and experience true freedom. It's a journey of transformation that will lead you to a life reflecting Christ's very heart. Are you ready to embrace the Spirit-empowered life that awaits you?

Chapter 1:
The Holy Spirit –
Our Source of Empowerment

We begin our journey towards a Spirit-empowered life by understanding the very source of that power: the Holy Spirit. He is not merely a force or an influence but the third person of the Trinity, co-equal with God the Father and God the Son. He is the one who empowers us to live out the grace, compassion, and forgiveness we so desperately need.

Who is the Holy Spirit?

The Bible reveals the Holy Spirit as a distinct person possessing intellect, will, and emotions. Jesus Himself referred to the Spirit as "he" (John 16:13), and throughout Scripture, we see the Spirit acting with intention and purpose. He convicts the world of sin (John 16:8), guides believers into truth (John 16:13), and empowers us for service (Acts 1:8).

The Holy Spirit is also described as the "Spirit of God" (Genesis 1:2), the "Spirit of Christ" (Romans 8:9), and the "Helper" or "Advocate" (John 14:16). These names reveal His intimate connection with the Father and the Son, and His active role in the lives of believers. He is the one who brings God's presence and power into our hearts, enabling us to live in a way that pleases Him.

Transformative Questions:

1. How does understanding the personhood of the Holy Spirit change your perspective on His role in your life?

   _____
   _____
   _____
   _____

2. In what ways have you experienced the Holy Spirit's presence and activity in your own life?

   _____
   _____
   _____
   _____

3. How can you cultivate a deeper awareness of the Holy Spirit's work within you?

   _____
   _____
   _____
   _____

The Role of the Spirit in Believers' Lives

The Holy Spirit plays a vital role in the lives of believers. He is the one who:

> Regenerates us: The Spirit gives us new life, bringing us from spiritual death to spiritual life (John 3:5-8).
>
> Indwells us: He takes up residence within us, making our bodies His temple (1 Corinthians 6:19).
>
> Empowers us: He gives us the strength and ability to live a godly life and fulfill our calling (Acts 1:8).
>
> Guides us: He leads us into truth and directs our paths (John 16:13).
>
> Comforts us: He provides peace and comfort in times of trouble (John 14:16).
>
> Produces fruit in us: He cultivates within us the character of Christ, such as love, joy, peace, patience, kindness, goodness, faithfulness, gentleness, and self-control (Galatians 5:22-23).

In short, the Holy Spirit is our constant companion, helper, and guide. He is the source of our strength, wisdom, and transformation.

Transformative Questions:

1. Which of these roles of the Holy Spirit resonates most with you right now, and why?

   _____
   _____
   _____
   _____

2. In what areas of your life do you need the Spirit's empowerment the most?

   _____
   _____
   _____
   _____

3. How can you actively seek the Spirit's guidance in your daily decisions and actions?

   _____
   _____
   _____
   _____

Sealed by the Spirit

Ephesians 1:13-14 tells us believers are "sealed with the promised Holy Spirit, who is a deposit guaranteeing our inheritance until the redemption of those who are God's possession." This sealing signifies our secure salvation and marks us as God's own. It guarantees that we belong to Him and that He will complete the work He has begun in us.

This sealing also has implications for our daily lives. Knowing that the Spirit seals us should give us confidence and boldness to live for Christ. It should motivate us to pursue holiness and resist the world's temptations. And it should remind us that we are not alone in our journey; the Holy Spirit is with us always, empowering us to live victoriously.

Transformative Questions:

1. How does the knowledge of being sealed by the Spirit affect your sense of security and identity in Christ?

   _____
   _____
   _____
   _____

2. In what ways does this truth empower you to live differently?

   _____
   _____
   _____
   _____

3. How can you remind yourself of this sealing when you face challenges or doubts?

   _____
   _____
   _____
   _____

Chapter 2:
Not Grieving the Holy Spirit – Maintaining a Spirit-Filled Heart

In the previous chapter, we explored the incredible gift of the Holy Spirit and His vital role in our lives. But this gift comes with a responsibility: not to grieve the Spirit. Ephesians 4:30 urges us, "And do not grieve the Holy Spirit of God, with whom you were sealed for the day of redemption." This verse calls us to a life of sensitivity and obedience to the Spirit's leading. But what does it actually mean to grieve the Holy Spirit? And what are the consequences of doing so?

What It Means to Grieve the Spirit

The Greek word translated as "grieve" in Ephesians 4:30 carries the idea of causing sorrow or pain. Just as we can grieve a loved one through our words or actions, we can also grieve the Holy Spirit. This happens when we:

> **Resist His leading:** The Spirit gently guides us through conviction, prompting, and intuition. When we ignore or resist His leading, we quench His work in our lives (1 Thessalonians 5:19).

Engage in sin: Sinful behavior directly contradicts the Spirit's work of sanctification within us. It creates a barrier between us and God, hindering our fellowship with Him (Isaiah 59:2).

Harbor unforgiveness: Unforgiveness, bitterness, and resentment create a breeding ground for negativity that stifles the Spirit's work and hinders our spiritual growth (Hebrews 12:15).

Live in disobedience: Willful disobedience to God's Word demonstrates a lack of respect for the Spirit's authority and guidance (1 Samuel 15:23).

Embrace worldly values: When we prioritize the things of this world over the things of God, we grieve the Spirit who desires our wholehearted devotion (1 John 2:15-17).

Essentially, grieving the Spirit occurs whenever we choose our own will over His, hindering His work in our lives and damaging our relationship with God.

Transformative Questions:

1. Which of these actions or attitudes do you struggle with the most?

   _____
   _____
   _____
   _____

2. How can you become more aware of the Spirit's promptings in your daily life?

   _____
   _____
   _____
   _____

3. What practical steps can you take to avoid grieving the Spirit in these areas?

   _____
   _____
   _____
   _____

Consequences of Grieving the Spirit

Grieving the Holy Spirit has significant consequences for our spiritual lives. It can lead to:

> **Loss of peace and joy:** When we grieve the Spirit, we disrupt our fellowship with God, leading to a sense of distance and unease (Galatians 5:22).
>
> **Hindered spiritual growth:** The Spirit is the agent of our transformation, but when we grieve Him, we stunt our spiritual development (2 Peter 3:18).
>
> **Weakened spiritual sensitivity:** Repeatedly ignoring the Spirit's promptings can dull our sensitivity to His voice, making it harder to discern His guidance (Hebrews 5:14).
>
> **Increased susceptibility to temptation:** When we grieve the Spirit, we weaken our defenses against sin, making us more vulnerable to the enemy's attacks (Ephesians 6:10-18).
>
> **Strained relationships:** A grieved Spirit can affect our interactions with others, leading to conflict, bitterness, and broken relationships (Ephesians 4:31-32).

Ultimately, grieving the Spirit hinders our ability to live the abundant life Jesus promised (John 10:10).

Transformative Questions:

1. Have you experienced any of these consequences in your own life?

   _____
   _____
   _____
   _____

2. How has grieving the Spirit affected your relationship with God and others?

   _____
   _____
   _____
   _____

3. What steps can you take to restore your fellowship with the Spirit and experience His fullness again?

   _____
   _____
   _____
   _____

Cultivating a Spirit-Filled Heart

Maintaining a Spirit-filled heart requires intentionality and a commitment to living harmoniously with the Spirit's leading. Here are some practical ways to cultivate a Spirit-filled life:

Prioritize prayer and Bible reading: Spending time in God's Word and in prayer keeps us connected to the source of our strength and guidance (Psalm 119:105, John 15:7).

Practice obedience: Responding promptly to the Spirit's promptings demonstrates our willingness to follow His lead (John 14:15).

Confess sin quickly: We should confess it immediately and seek forgiveness, restoring our fellowship with God (1 John 1:9).

Cultivate gratitude: A grateful heart focuses on God's goodness and fosters an attitude that pleases the Spirit (1 Thessalonians 5:18).

Surround yourself with godly influences: Spending time with other believers seeking to live Spirit-filled lives encourages and strengthens our own walk with God (Hebrews 10:24-25).

Be mindful of your thoughts and attitudes: Negativity, complaining, and critical thoughts can quench the Spirit's work. Instead, focus on true, noble, right, pure, lovely, admirable, excellent, and praiseworthy (Philippians 4:8).

By consistently practicing these disciplines, we create an environment where the Spirit can freely work in our lives, producing the fruit of His presence and empowering us to live a life of grace, compassion, and forgiveness.

Transformative Questions:

1. Which of these practices do you need to focus on developing?

   _____
   _____
   _____
   _____

2. What specific steps can you take to incorporate these practices into your daily routine?

   _____
   _____
   _____
   _____

3. How can you create an atmosphere in your life that is conducive to the Spirit's presence and work?

   _____
   _____
   _____
   _____

Chapter 3:
Letting Go – Releasing Bitterness, Anger, and Malice

In pursuing a Spirit-empowered life, we encounter a significant obstacle: the weight of negative emotions. Ephesians 4:31 vividly depicts these inner burdens: "Get rid of all bitterness, rage and anger, brawling and slander, along with every form of malice." These destructive emotions not only hinder our spiritual growth but also poison our relationships and rob us of true freedom. This chapter explores the damaging effects of these emotions and provides practical steps, empowered by the Spirit, to release them and embrace emotional and spiritual healing.

The Weight of Negative Emotions

Negative emotions like bitterness, rage, anger, brawling, slander, and malice act as heavy weights, dragging us down and hindering our progress in the Christian life. Let's examine the specific impact of each:

> **Bitterness:** This deep-seated resentment festers within, poisoning our thoughts and actions. It focuses on past hurts, preventing us from moving forward and experiencing forgiveness and healing (Hebrews 12:15).

Rage and Anger: These explosive emotions erupt in destructive ways, damaging relationships and creating a hostile environment. Uncontrolled anger can lead to rash decisions, hurtful words, and physical violence (Proverbs 29:22).

Brawling: This contentious spirit thrives on conflict and discord. It stirs up strife, creates division, and disrupts the peace and unity that should characterize Christian communities (Proverbs 20:3).

Slander: This malicious use of words tears down others and spreads harmful gossip. It destroys reputations, breeds mistrust, and creates a toxic atmosphere (Proverbs 10:18).

Malice: This deep-seated ill will desires to harm others. It manifests in acts of revenge, sabotage, and cruelty, poisoning our hearts and hindering our ability to love (1 Corinthians 13:4-7).

These negative emotions create a barrier between us and God, hindering our spiritual growth and preventing us from experiencing the fullness of His love and grace. They weigh us down, keeping us captive to the past and robbing us of the freedom and joy that are ours in Christ.

Transformative Questions:

1. Which of these negative emotions do you struggle with the most?

   _____
   _____
   _____
   _____

2. How have these emotions affected your relationships and your spiritual well-being?

   _____
   _____
   _____
   _____

3. What are the root causes of these emotions in your life?

   _____
   _____
   _____
   _____

Spiritual and Emotional Freedom

Releasing these negative emotions is essential for experiencing true spiritual and emotional freedom. When we let go of bitterness, anger, and malice, we open ourselves to the transformative work of the Holy Spirit. This freedom brings:

> **Peace and Joy:** Letting go of negativity allows us to experience the peace that surpasses all understanding and the joy that comes from a close relationship with God (Philippians 4:7, John 15:11).
>
> **Improved Relationships:** Releasing bitterness and anger paves the way for reconciliation and healing in our relationships. It allows us to extend forgiveness and experience the joy of restored connections (Colossians 3:13).
>
> **Spiritual Growth:** When we are free from the weight of negative emotions, we can focus on pursuing God and growing in our faith. We become more receptive to the Spirit's leading and more fruitful in our Christian walk (Galatians 5:22-23).
>
> **Emotional Healing:** Letting go of past hurts and resentments allows us to experience emotional healing and wholeness. We can break free from the cycle of pain and embrace a future filled with hope and freedom (Psalm 34:18).
>
> **Greater Capacity for Love:** When we release malice and embrace forgiveness, we create space in our hearts for love to

flourish. We become more like Christ, who loved us unconditionally and forgave us freely (Ephesians 4:32).

The freedom that comes from releasing negative emotions is a precious gift. It allows us to live more fully, love more deeply, and experience the abundant life that Jesus promised.

Transformative Questions:

1. How would your life be different if you were free from the burden of these negative emotions?

   _____
   _____
   _____
   _____

2. What areas of your life would be most impacted by this freedom?

   _____
   _____
   _____
   _____

3. What steps can you take to embrace this freedom and experience its benefits?

   _____
   _____
   _____
   _____

Practical Steps to Let Go

Letting go of negative emotions is not always easy, but it is possible with the help of the Holy Spirit. Here are some practical steps to help you release bitterness, anger, and malice:

Acknowledge and identify the emotions: The first step towards healing is recognizing and naming the specific emotions you are experiencing. Be honest about the hurt, anger, or resentment you are holding onto.

Pray for God's help: Ask the Holy Spirit to reveal these emotions' root causes and give you the strength to let go. Surrender your hurt and anger to Him, trusting Him to bring healing and restoration (Philippians 4:6-7).

Forgive those who have hurt you: Forgiveness is a powerful act of releasing bitterness and anger. Choose to forgive, even when it's difficult, remembering that Christ forgave you (Ephesians 4:32).

Replace negative thoughts with positive ones: When negative thoughts arise, combat them with truth from God's Word. Focus on God's love, promises, and faithfulness (Philippians 4:8).

Practice gratitude: Cultivating gratitude shifts your focus from what you lack to what you have. Thankfulness counteracts negativity and opens your heart to God's blessings (1 Thessalonians 5:18).

Seek support from others: Talk to a trusted friend, mentor, or counselor about your struggles. Sharing your burdens with others can provide encouragement, accountability, and support on your journey toward healing (Galatians 6:2).

Letting go of negative emotions is a process, not a one-time event. Be patient with yourself, and rely on the Holy Spirit's power to transform your heart and mind. As you choose to let go, you will experience the freedom and joy of living a Spirit-empowered life.

Transformative Questions:

1. Which of these steps resonates most with you right now?

   _____
   _____
   _____
   _____

2. What specific actions can you take to implement these steps in your life?

   _____
   _____
   _____
   _____

3. Who can you contact for support and accountability as you work towards releasing negative emotions?

   _____
   _____
   _____
   _____

Chapter 4:
Embracing Grace – Cultivating Kindness and Compassion

Having explored the freedom of releasing negative emotions, we now focus on cultivating positive qualities that mark a Spirit-empowered life. Ephesians 4:32 instructs us to "be kind and compassionate to one another, forgiving each other, just as in Christ God forgave you." This chapter delves into the transformative power of kindness and compassion, exploring how these virtues shape our relationships, communities, and our own spiritual well-being.

The Power of Kindness

Kindness, often seen as a simple act, holds immense power to transform lives and communities. It is an active expression of love, demonstrating care and consideration for others. The power of kindness lies in its ability to:

> **Build bridges:** Kindness transcends differences and fosters connection. A simple act of kindness can break down barriers, heal wounds, and open doors to meaningful relationships (Proverbs 18:24).

> **Encourage and uplift:** A kind word or gesture can brighten someone's day and offer encouragement in times of dif-

ficulty. Kindness has the power to inspire hope and instill a sense of belonging (1 Thessalonians 5:11).

Create a ripple effect: Kindness is contagious. When we experience kindness, we are more likely to extend it to others, creating a ripple effect that spreads positivity and goodwill (Galatians 6:10).

Reflect God's love: Ultimately, kindness reflects God's own character. When we are kind to others, we demonstrate His love and compassion for a world in need (Ephesians 5:1).

Kindness is not merely a suggestion; it is a command. As followers of Christ, we are called to be agents of kindness, reflecting His love and transforming the world around us.

Transformative Questions:

1. How have you experienced the power of kindness in your own life?

   _____
   _____
   _____
   _____

2. Who in your life has demonstrated kindness to you in a meaningful way?

   _____
   _____
   _____
   _____

3. How can you be more intentional about showing kindness to others?

   _____
   _____
   _____
   _____

Deepening Compassion

Compassion goes beyond kindness; it is a deep empathy that moves us to action. It is the ability to understand and share the feelings of others, particularly their suffering. Developing compassion requires:

> **Cultivating empathy:** Empathy involves putting ourselves in another person's shoes, and seeking to understand their perspective and emotions. It requires active listening, genuine curiosity, and a willingness to see the world through their eyes (Romans 12:15).
>
> **Opening our hearts:** Compassion requires a willingness to be vulnerable and allow ourselves to be affected by the pain and needs of others. It means moving beyond indifference and engaging with the suffering around us (1 Peter 3:8).
>
> **Following Christ's example:** Jesus was the ultimate example of compassion. His compassion for others moved him, and he actively sought to heal, comfort, and restore. We deepen our compassion by studying His life and striving to emulate His example (Matthew 9:36).

Compassion is not a passive emotion; it compels us to act. It motivates us to reach out to those in need, offer support, and work towards alleviating suffering.

Transformative Questions:

1. What hinders you from experiencing more profound compassion for others?

   _____
   _____
   _____
   _____

2. How can you cultivate greater empathy and understanding in your relationships?

   _____
   _____
   _____
   _____

3. In what ways can you actively demonstrate compassion to those in need?

   _____
   _____
   _____
   _____

Spirit-Led Acts of Grace

The Holy Spirit empowers us to live out kindness and compassion practically. He guides us to opportunities to serve, provides the strength to act, and inspires creative expressions of grace. Here are some examples of Spirit-led acts of grace:

Offering a helping hand: Look for ways to assist those in need, whether helping a neighbor with chores, offering a ride to someone without transportation, or volunteering at a local charity (Galatians 6:2).

Speaking words of encouragement: Offer affirmation, support, and hope to those struggling. A kind word can significantly impact someone's life (Proverbs 12:25).

Extending forgiveness: Forgiveness is an act of grace that releases both the offender and the offended from bitterness and resentment. Choose to forgive, even when difficult, demonstrating the same grace Christ extended to you (Colossians 3:13).

Practicing hospitality: Open your home and your heart to others. Welcome strangers, invite friends for a meal and create a space where people feel loved and accepted (Romans 12:13).

Giving generously: Share your resources with those in need. Whether it's financial support, donating goods, or offering your time and talents, generosity is a tangible expression of compassion (2 Corinthians 9:7).

These are just a few examples of how we can demonstrate kindness and compassion daily. The Holy Spirit will lead you to specific opportunities to be an agent of grace in your unique context. Be sensitive to His promptings and willing to act in obedience.

Transformative Questions:

1. Which of these acts of grace resonates most with you?

   _____
   _____
   _____
   _____

2. What specific opportunities do you have to demonstrate kindness and compassion daily?

   _____
   _____
   _____
   _____

3. How can you be more attentive to the Spirit's leading in expressing grace to others?

   _____
   _____
   _____
   _____

Chapter 5:
The Art of Forgiveness – Reflecting Christ's Forgiveness

Forgiveness is a cornerstone of the Christian faith, a radical act of love that mirrors God's very heart. In Ephesians 4:32, we are called to forgive "just as in Christ God forgave you." This chapter delves into the profound concept of biblical forgiveness, exploring its theological foundation, the unparalleled example set by Christ, and practical strategies for overcoming the barriers that often hinder us from extending forgiveness to others.

Understanding Biblical Forgiveness

In its truest sense, forgiveness is not merely forgetting or excusing an offense. It is a deliberate and conscious choice to release resentment and the desire for revenge, offering grace and mercy instead. Biblical forgiveness involves:

> **Acknowledging the offense:** Forgiveness begins with recognizing the wrong committed and the pain it has caused. It requires honesty and a willingness to confront the reality of the situation (Luke 17:3-4).
>
> **Releasing the debt:** Forgiveness involves relinquishing the right to demand justice or retribution. It is a decision

to cancel the debt owed to us, just as God canceled our debt through Christ (Matthew 6:12).

Choosing to love: Forgiveness is an act of love, motivated by a desire for reconciliation and restoration. It is a choice to extend grace and mercy, even when it is undeserved (Colossians 3:13).

Trusting God for justice: Forgiveness does not mean condoning wrongdoing or ignoring the consequences of sin. It involves trusting God to bring justice and healing in His own way and time (Romans 12:19).

Biblical forgiveness is a powerful force that breaks the cycle of bitterness and resentment, paving the way for healing and reconciliation. It is a reflection of God's own character and a testament to the transformative power of His grace.

Transformative Questions:

1. How does this understanding of biblical forgiveness differ from your previous perception of forgiveness?

   _____
   _____
   _____
   _____

2. What aspects of biblical forgiveness do you find most challenging?

   _____
   _____
   _____
   _____

3. How can you deepen your understanding of forgiveness as an act of love and grace?

   _____
   _____
   _____
   _____

Christ as Our Example

Jesus Christ is the ultimate example of forgiveness. On the cross, He forgave those who crucified Him, demonstrating the boundless love and mercy of God (Luke 23:34). His example teaches us:

> **Forgiveness is unconditional:** Jesus offered forgiveness freely without requiring anything in return. He did not wait for repentance or apologies; He simply forgave (Romans 5:8).
>
> **Forgiveness is sacrificial:** Forgiveness cost Jesus everything. He endured unimaginable suffering and death on the cross to make forgiveness possible for us (1 Peter 2:24).
>
> **Forgiveness is transformative:** Jesus' forgiveness released those who crucified Him from their guilt and opened the door for them to experience new life in Him (John 3:16).

Christ's example challenges us to extend forgiveness even in difficult circumstances. He shows us that forgiveness is not a sign of weakness but an act of extraordinary love and strength.

Transformative Questions:

1. How does Jesus' example on the cross inspire you to forgive others?

   _____
   _____
   _____
   _____

2. What specific aspects of Jesus' forgiveness do you find most compelling?

   _____
   _____
   _____
   _____

3. How can you reflect Christ's example of forgiveness in your own relationships?

   _____
   _____
   _____
   _____

Overcoming Barriers to Forgiveness

While forgiveness is a powerful force for healing, it is often hindered by various barriers. These barriers may include:

> **Pride:** Pride makes it difficult to admit we have been wronged and to acknowledge our need for forgiveness. It can also make us unwilling to extend forgiveness to others (Proverbs 16:18).
>
> **Fear:** Fear of vulnerability, rejection, or further hurt can prevent us from forgiving. We may fear that forgiveness will be seen as weakness or will allow the offender to hurt us again (1 John 4:18).
>
> **Unresolved pain:** Deep emotional wounds can make it difficult to release resentment and anger. Unresolved pain can keep us trapped in a cycle of bitterness and unforgiveness (Psalm 34:18).

Overcoming these barriers requires the empowering work of the Holy Spirit. He can:

> **Soften our hearts:** The Spirit can break down the walls of pride and fear, enabling us to acknowledge our need for forgiveness and to extend it to others (Ezekiel 36:26).
>
> **Heal our wounds:** The Spirit can comfort and heal our emotional wounds, enabling us to release the pain and resentment that hinder forgiveness (Psalm 147:3).

Empower us to love: The Spirit can fill us with God's love, enabling us to forgive even those who have deeply hurt us (Romans 5:5).

By relying on the Spirit's power, we can overcome the barriers that prevent us from forgiving and experience the freedom and healing that forgiveness brings.

Transformative Questions:

1. What barriers to forgiveness do you struggle with the most?

   _____
   _____
   _____
   _____

2. How can you rely on the Holy Spirit to overcome these barriers?

   _____
   _____
   _____
   _____

3. What practical steps can you take to cultivate a forgiving heart?

   _____
   _____
   _____
   _____

Chapter 6:
Living in Harmony – Building Unified Communities

While the previous chapters focused on personal transformation, this chapter expands our vision to encompass the broader community. Ephesians 4:32 doesn't just call us to individual acts of kindness and forgiveness; it speaks to a collective transformation that fosters unity and harmony within our families, churches, and communities. This chapter explores the Holy Spirit's role in building unified communities, the power of forgiveness to heal relationships, and practical steps toward creating a culture of compassion.

The Role of the Holy Spirit in Community

The Holy Spirit is the unifying force within the Christian community. He transcends our differences, binds us in love, and empowers us to live harmoniously. The Spirit fosters unity by:

> **Creating a shared identity:** The Spirit baptizes us into one body, making us members of Christ and heirs to His promises (1 Corinthians 12:13). This shared identity transcends our backgrounds, cultures, and personalities, uniting us in Christ.
>
> **Gifting us for service:** The Spirit equips each believer with unique gifts to build up the body (1 Corinthians 12:7).

When we use our gifts to serve one another, we contribute to the health and growth of the community.

Producing spiritual fruit: The fruit of the Spirit—love, joy, peace, patience, kindness, goodness, faithfulness, gentleness, and self-control—are essential for harmonious community living (Galatians 5:22-23). These qualities foster understanding, cooperation, and mutual respect.

Empowering us to love: Love is the defining characteristic of the Christian community (John 13:35). The Spirit pours God's love into our hearts, enabling us to love one another unconditionally, even when it's difficult (Romans 5:5).

The Spirit's presence in the community creates an atmosphere of belonging, acceptance, and mutual support. It empowers us to overcome our differences, work together towards common goals, and reflect God's love to the world.

Transformative Questions:

1. How have you experienced the Holy Spirit's unifying work in your community?

   _____
   _____
   _____
   _____

2. How can you contribute to building unity within your family, church, or community?

   _____
   _____
   _____
   _____

3. How can you better utilize your spiritual gifts to serve others and strengthen the body of Christ?

   _____
   _____
   _____
   _____

Healing Relationships through Forgiveness

Forgiveness is crucial in healing broken relationships and restoring harmony within communities. When offenses occur, forgiveness breaks the cycle of bitterness and resentment, allowing for reconciliation and renewed connection. Forgiveness in the community:

Restores trust: When we forgive, we demonstrate a willingness to move forward, offering a second chance and rebuilding trust that may have been broken (Ephesians 4:32).

Promotes healing: Forgiveness releases both the offender and the offended from the grip of pain and anger, allowing for emotional healing and restoration (Colossians 3:13).

Strengthens bonds: Forgiveness creates an opportunity for deeper connection and understanding. It allows relationships to grow stronger, built on a foundation of grace and mercy (Matthew 18:21-22).

Models Christ's love: When we forgive one another, we reflect Christ's forgiving love to the world. This powerful witness can draw others to Him and inspire them to experience the same transformative power of forgiveness (1 John 4:19).

Forgiveness is not always easy, but it is essential for building healthy and thriving communities. It requires humility, compassion, and a willingness to let go of the past.

Transformative Questions:

1. How has forgiveness played a role in healing relationships within your own community?

   _____
   _____
   _____
   _____

2. What steps can you take to promote a culture of forgiveness within your family or church?

   _____
   _____
   _____
   _____

3. How can you be an ambassador of forgiveness, modeling Christ's love to those around you?

   _____
   _____
   _____
   _____

Creating a Compassionate Culture

Building a compassionate culture requires a collective commitment to embracing kindness and forgiveness. It involves creating an environment where people feel valued, supported, and empowered to grow. Here are some practical steps toward creating a compassionate culture:

Promote empathy and understanding: Encourage active listening, perspective-taking, and genuine curiosity about others' experiences. Create open dialogue and sharing spaces, fostering a deeper understanding of one another's needs and challenges (Romans 12:10).

Celebrate diversity: Recognize and appreciate each person's unique gifts and perspectives to the community. Embrace diversity as a strength, fostering a sense of belonging and inclusivity (1 Corinthians 12:12-27).

Practice servant leadership: Leaders should model compassion, humility, and a willingness to serve others. Create a culture where leadership empowers others, fosters growth, and meets needs (Matthew 20:26-28).

Offer support and encouragement: Be quick to offer help, encouragement, and support to those struggling. Create systems of care and accountability that ensure everyone feels seen and valued (Galatians 6:2).

Promote restorative justice: When conflicts arise, seek solutions focusing on restoration and reconciliation rather than punishment. Create opportunities for dialogue, forgiveness, and healing, fostering a sense of justice and fairness within the community (Matthew 5:23-24).

Creating a compassionate culture is an ongoing process that requires intentionality and commitment from every community member. By embracing kindness, forgiveness, and a spirit of unity, we can create a thriving community that reflects the love of Christ.

Transformative Questions:

1. What are some specific ways your community can foster a more compassionate culture?

   _____
   _____
   _____
   _____

2. How can you personally contribute to creating an environment of kindness and forgiveness?

   _____
   _____
   _____
   _____

3. What steps can your community take to support better those who are struggling or marginalized?

   _____
   _____
   _____
   _____

Chapter 7:
Daily Empowerment – Walking in the Spirit

Throughout this book, we've explored the transformative power of the Holy Spirit in cultivating grace, compassion, and forgiveness. But how do we maintain this Spirit-empowered life day in and day out? This chapter focuses on the practicalities of walking in the Spirit, embracing spiritual disciplines that keep us connected to Him, surrendering to His leading in every aspect of life, and ultimately becoming vessels of His love to a world in desperate need.

Spiritual Disciplines for Empowerment

Spiritual disciplines are intentional practices that cultivate our relationship with God and create space for the Spirit to work. They are not merely rituals or routines but pathways to deeper intimacy with God and greater empowerment to live Christ-centered lives. Some key spiritual disciplines include:

> **Prayer:** Prayer is our lifeline to God, a conversation in which we express our adoration, confess our shortcomings, seek His guidance, and intercede for others (Philippians 4:6). Consistent prayer keeps us connected to the source of our strength and aligns our hearts with His will.

Bible Reading and Meditation: Immersing ourselves in God's Word nourishes our souls, renews our minds, and reveals His character and purposes (Psalm 119:105). Meditation allows us to ponder Scripture deeply, allowing its truths to penetrate our hearts and transform our thinking.

Fasting: Fasting involves abstaining from food or other physical comforts for a designated period to focus on prayer and seeking God's face (Matthew 6:16-18). It cultivates spiritual hunger, deepens our dependence on God, and increases our sensitivity to His voice.

Worship: Worship is an expression of our love and devotion to God. Through singing, praising, and expressing gratitude, we acknowledge His greatness and surrender our hearts to Him (Psalm 95:1-7). Worship invites the Spirit's presence and fills us with His joy and peace.

Solitude and Silence: Creating space for solitude and silence allows us to quiet the world's noise and listen for the still, small voice of the Spirit (Psalm 46:10). In these moments of stillness, we can reflect on God's Word, examine our hearts, and receive His guidance.

These disciplines, practiced regularly, create a fertile ground for the Spirit to work in our lives, empowering us to live out the grace, compassion, and forgiveness we have been exploring.

Transformative Questions:

1. Which spiritual disciplines are already a part of your life?

   _____
   _____
   _____
   _____

2. Which disciplines do you need to cultivate or strengthen?

   _____
   _____
   _____
   _____

3. How can you create space in your daily routine for these practices?

   _____
   _____
   _____
   _____

Daily Surrender and Dependence

Walking in the Spirit requires a posture of daily surrender and dependence. It means recognizing our own limitations and relying on the Spirit's power to guide, strengthen, and transform us. This involves:

> **Acknowledging our need:** We must recognize that we cannot live the Christian life in our own strength. We need the Spirit's constant help to overcome temptation, make wise choices, and fulfill God's purposes (John 15:5).

> **Surrendering our will:** Surrender involves yielding our desires, plans, and ambitions to God's will. It means trusting His wisdom and allowing Him to lead us, even when His plans differ from our own (Proverbs 3:5-6).

> **Seeking His guidance in all things:** Whether facing major decisions or navigating everyday challenges, we should seek the Spirit's guidance through prayer, Scripture, and wise counsel (James 1:5).

> **Obeying His promptings:** When the Spirit speaks to our hearts, we must be willing to obey, even when it requires stepping outside our comfort zones or going against the grain of the world (John 14:15).

Daily surrender and dependence are not one-time events but a continual process of yielding to the Spirit's leading and trusting Him to work in and through us.

Transformative Questions:

1. In what areas of your life do you struggle to surrender control to the Holy Spirit?

   _____
   _____
   _____
   _____

2. How can you cultivate a greater dependence on the Spirit in your daily life?

   _____
   _____
   _____
   _____

3. What practical steps can you take to be more attentive to the Spirit's promptings and obedient to His leading?

   _____
   _____
   _____
   _____

Living as a Vessel of the Spirit

As we walk in the Spirit, we become vessels through which God's love, grace, and forgiveness flow to a broken world. This means:

> **Reflecting Christ's character:** The Spirit transforms us from the inside out, conforming us to the image of Christ (2 Corinthians 3:18). As we become more like Him, we naturally radiate His love, grace, and compassion to those around us.
>
> **Sharing the Gospel:** The Spirit empowers us to be bold witnesses for Christ, sharing the good news of salvation with those who need to hear it (Acts 1:8). We become conduits of His grace, offering hope and healing to a hurting world.
>
> **Serving others:** The Spirit equips us with unique gifts and talents to serve others and build up the body of Christ (1 Peter 4:10). We become channels of His love, meeting needs, offering support, and demonstrating compassion practically.
>
> **Extending forgiveness:** As we have received forgiveness from God, we are called to extend forgiveness to others (Ephesians 4:32). We become instruments of His grace, breaking the cycle of bitterness and resentment and promoting reconciliation.

Living as a vessel of the Spirit is a high calling, requiring humility, obedience, and a willingness to be used by God for His purposes. It is a life of purpose and impact, bringing glory to God and making a difference in the world.

Transformative Questions:

1. How can you be a more effective vessel of God's love, grace, and forgiveness in your daily interactions?

   _____
   _____
   _____
   _____

2. What opportunities do you have to share the Gospel and be a witness for Christ?

   _____
   _____
   _____
   _____

3. How can you use your gifts and talents to serve others and build up the body of Christ?

   _____
   _____
   _____
   _____

Conclusion:
A Spirit-Empowered Journey of Transformation

As we conclude this journey through the pages of "Spirit Empowered," let's recap the key principles we've uncovered and embrace the ongoing adventure of living a life transformed by the Holy Spirit.

We began by recognizing our deep need for the Spirit's empowerment. Ephesians 4:30-32 calls us to a life transcending our natural inclinations: a life of kindness, compassion, and forgiveness. But we quickly realized that such a life is impossible in our own strength. We need the Holy Spirit to break the chains of negativity, heal our wounded hearts, and empower us to love as Christ loves.

Throughout this book, we've explored the multifaceted work of the Holy Spirit in our lives. He is the source of our strength, our guide into truth, and the one who produces within us the very character of Christ. We've learned to recognize His voice, avoid grieving Him, and cultivate a Spirit-filled heart. We've discovered the freedom from releasing bitterness, anger, and malice and embraced the transformative power of grace, compassion, and forgiveness.

But this is not a destination; it's an ongoing journey. The Christian life is a continual process of growth, surrender, and dependence on the Holy Spirit. We will face challenges, stumble sometimes, and must continually realign our hearts with God's will. But the good news is that the Holy Spirit is always with us, empowering us to persevere, grow, and become more like Christ.

A Call to Action:

Now is the time to fully embrace the Spirit-empowered life that awaits you. Surrender your heart to Him, allowing Him to lead you into a life of greater freedom, purpose, and impact. Commit to cultivating the spiritual disciplines that keep you connected to Him, and be bold in demonstrating His love, grace, and forgiveness to a world in need.

Transformative Questions:

What specific steps will you take to cultivate a deeper relationship with the Holy Spirit? (John 14:26 - "But the Advocate, the Holy Spirit, whom the Father will send in my name, will teach you all things and will remind you of everything I have said to you.")

_____
_____
_____
_____

How will you practically demonstrate grace, compassion, and forgiveness daily? (Colossians 3:12 - "Therefore, as God's chosen people, holy and dearly loved, clothe yourselves with compassion, kindness, humility, gentleness, and patience.")

_____
_____

_____

_____

How will you allow the Holy Spirit to use you as a vessel of His love for the world? (1 Peter 4:10 - "Each of you should use whatever gift you have received to serve others, as faithful stewards of God's grace in its various forms.")

_____

_____

_____

_____

May you walk in the fullness of the Spirit's power, experiencing the abundant life that Jesus promised and making a lasting impact for His Kingdom.

Dear Reader,

Have you ever longed to hear God's voice more clearly? To experience His guidance in your daily life? To walk in the fullness of His power and purpose?

This 30-day Challenge, Intentionally Listening to the Spirit, is designed to help you do just that. It's an invitation to cultivate a deeper relationship with the Holy Spirit, the third person of the Trinity who dwells within every believer.

Why embark on this challenge? Here's what you stand to gain:

> **Intimacy with God:** Jesus promised, "But the Advocate, the Holy Spirit, whom the Father will send in my name, will teach you all things and will remind you of everything I have said to you" (John 14:26). Through this challenge, you'll create space to encounter the Spirit and experience the intimate fellowship He offers.
>
> **Guidance and Direction:** The Spirit is our guide, leading us into all truth. "But when he, the Spirit of truth, comes, he will guide you into all the truth" (John 16:13). Tuning your heart to His voice will give you clarity and direction in life.
>
> **Spiritual Growth:** The Spirit empowers us to live a life that pleases God. "For those who the Spirit of God leads are the children of God" (Romans 8:14). This challenge will help you cultivate the fruit of the Spirit – love, joy, peace, patience, kindness, goodness, faithfulness, gentleness, and self-control (Galatians 5:22-23).

Freedom and Power: The Spirit breaks the chains of sin and empowers us to live victoriously. "Now the Lord is the Spirit, and where the Spirit of the Lord is, there is freedom" (2 Corinthians 3:17). Through this challenge, you'll experience greater freedom from fear, doubt, and the world's weight.

Purpose and Fulfillment: The Spirit equips us to fulfill God's unique calling for our lives. "Each of you should use whatever gift you have received to serve others, as faithful stewards of God's grace in its various forms" (1 Peter 4:10). This challenge will help you discover and walk in your God-given purpose.

This 30-Day Challenge is more than just a religious exercise. It's an opportunity to encounter the living God and experience the transformative power of His Spirit. Are you ready to embark on this adventure?

With anticipation,
Your Sister In Christ

Dear Reader,

Congratulations on taking this bold step to intentionally cultivate a deeper relationship with the Holy Spirit! This 30-day challenge is an invitation to tune your heart to His voice, to recognize His presence, and to experience His empowering work in your life.

As you embark on this journey, remember that the Holy Spirit is eager to meet you. He longs to guide, comfort, and reveal God's truth to you in profound ways. Be expectant, open, and willing to listen and obey.

Each day, as you meditate on the Scripture and reflect on the transformative question, create space for the Spirit to speak. Journal your thoughts, prayers, and any insights that arise. This is a journey of discovery, and the Holy Spirit is your guide.

Don't be discouraged if some days feel more challenging than others. The key is consistency. Even a few minutes each day can make a significant difference.

I'm praying for you as you begin this journey. May you encounter the Holy Spirit in fresh and powerful ways!

With you in the adventure,
Your Sister in Christ

30-Day Challenge: Intentionally Listening to the Spirit

This 30-day challenge is designed to help you tune your heart to the voice of the Holy Spirit and begin experiencing His empowering presence in your life. Each day, you'll find a scripture to meditate on and a transformative question to ponder. Take some time each day to reflect on the verse and question, allowing the Holy Spirit to speak to your heart.

Day 1: John 14:26 - "But the Advocate, the Holy Spirit, whom the Father will send in my name, will teach you all things and remind you of everything I have said to you."

Question: What are some ways the Holy Spirit has been teaching you lately?

Day 2: John 16:13 - "But when he, the Spirit of truth, comes, he will guide you into all the truth. He will not speak on his own; he will speak only what he hears and tell you what is yet to come."

Question: How can you be more open to the Spirit's guidance?

Day 3: Romans 8:14 - "For those who the Spirit of God leads are the children of God."

Question: What does it mean to be led by the Spirit in your everyday life?

_____
_____
_____
_____
_____
_____
_____
_____
_____
_____
_____
_____
_____
_____
_____
_____
_____
_____
_____
_____
_____
_____
_____
_____

Day 4: Romans 8:26 - "Similarly, the Spirit helps us in our weakness. We do not know what we ought to pray for, but the Spirit himself intercedes for us through wordless groans."

Question: How can you rely on the Spirit's help in your prayer life?

Day 5: 1 Corinthians 2:10-11 - "But God has revealed it to us by his Spirit. The Spirit searches all things, even the deep things of God. For who knows a person's thoughts except their own spirit within them? In the same way, no one knows the thoughts of God except the Spirit of God."

Question: How does the Spirit help you understand God's truth?

_____
_____
_____
_____
_____
_____
_____
_____
_____
_____
_____
_____
_____
_____
_____
_____
_____
_____
_____
_____

Day 6: 1 Corinthians 2:14 - "The person without the Spirit does not accept the things that come from the Spirit of God but considers them foolishness, and cannot understand them because they are discerned only through the Spirit."

Question: How can you cultivate a greater sensitivity to spiritual things?

Day 7: 1 Corinthians 3:16 - "Don't you know that you are God's temple and that God's Spirit dwells in your midst?"

Question: How does knowing that you are God's temple affect your choices and actions?

Day 8: 1 Corinthians 6:19 - "Do you not know that your bodies are temples of the Holy Spirit, who is in you, whom you have received from God? You are not your own;"

Question: How can you honor God with your body as a temple of the Holy Spirit?

Day 9: 2 Corinthians 3:17 - "Now the Lord is the Spirit, and where the Spirit of the Lord is, there is freedom."

Question: What areas of your life need the Spirit's freedom?

Day 10: Galatians 5:16 - "So I say, walk by the Spirit, and you will not gratify the desires of the flesh."

Question: How can you practically walk by the Spirit daily?

Day 11: Galatians 5:18 - "But if you are led by the Spirit, you are not under the law."

Question: What does it mean to be led by the Spirit rather than by legalism?

_____
_____
_____
_____
_____
_____
_____
_____
_____
_____
_____
_____
_____
_____
_____
_____
_____
_____
_____
_____
_____
_____
_____

Day 12: Galatians 5:22-23 - "But the fruit of the Spirit is love, joy, peace, forbearance, kindness, goodness, faithfulness, gentleness and self-control. Against such things, there is no law."

Question: Which fruit of the Spirit are you most aware of? Which do you need to cultivate more?

Day 13: Galatians 5:25 - "Since we live by the Spirit, let us keep in step with the Spirit."

Question: How can you stay in step with the Spirit's leading?

___
___
___
___
___
___
___
___
___
___
___
___
___
___
___
___
___
___
___
___
___
___
___

Day 14: Ephesians 1:13-14 - "And you also were included in Christ when you heard the message of truth, the gospel of your salvation. When you believed, you were marked in him with a seal, the promised Holy Spirit, a deposit guaranteeing our inheritance until the redemption of those who are God's possession—to the praise of his glory."

Question: How does knowing the Holy Spirit seals you impact your daily life?

Day 15: Ephesians 4:30 - "And do not grieve the Holy Spirit of God, with whom you were sealed for the day of redemption."

Question: What are some ways you might be grieving the Holy Spirit?

_____
_____
_____
_____
_____
_____
_____
_____
_____
_____
_____
_____
_____
_____
_____
_____
_____
_____
_____
_____
_____
_____
_____
_____
_____

Halfway Through

Dear Reader,

You're halfway there! How is the journey going so far?

I hope you're discovering the incredible joy of intentionally listening to the Holy Spirit. Perhaps you're noticing His gentle promptings more readily or experiencing a more profound sense of peace and purpose. Whatever your experience, keep pressing on!

Remember, this is a marathon, not a sprint. Some days feel easier than others. There might be times when you feel distant from God or struggle to hear His voice. That's okay. Don't give up. Keep seeking Him, listening, and trusting that He is at work in your life.

I'm cheering you on as you continue this journey. May the second half of this challenge be even more fruitful than the first!

In His grip,

Your Sister in Christ

Day 16: Ephesians 5:18 - "Do not get drunk on wine, which leads to debauchery. Instead, be filled with the Spirit,"

Question: How can you be filled with the Spirit daily?

Day 17: Philippians 2:13 - "For it is God who works in you to will and to act in order to fulfill his good purpose."

Question: How can you cooperate with God's work in your life?

Day 18: Colossians 1:9-10 - "For this reason, since we heard about you, we have not stopped praying for you. We continually ask God to fill you with the knowledge of his will through all the wisdom and understanding that the Spirit gives so that you may live a life worthy of the Lord and please him in every way: bearing fruit in every good work, growing in the knowledge of God,"

Question: How can you grow in your knowledge of God's will?

Day 19: 1 Thessalonians 5:19 - "Do not quench the Spirit."

Question: How can we quench the Spirit's work in our lives?

Day 20: 2 Timothy 1:7 - "For the Spirit God gave us does not make us timid, but gives us power, love and self-discipline."

Question: How can you access the power, love, and self-discipline the Spirit provides?

Day 21: Hebrews 3:7-11 - "So, as the Holy Spirit says: 'Today, if you hear his voice, do not harden your hearts as you did in the rebellion, during the time of testing in the wilderness, where your ancestors tested and tried me, though for forty years they saw what I did. That is why I was angry with that generation; I said, 'Their hearts are always going astray, and they have not known my ways.' So I declared on oath in my anger, 'They shall never enter my rest.'"

Question: How can you ensure you are not hardening your heart to the Spirit's voice?

Day 22: Hebrews 10:29 - "How much more severely do you think someone deserves to be punished who has trampled the Son of God underfoot, who has treated as an unholy thing the blood of the covenant that sanctified them, and who has insulted the Spirit of grace?"

Question: How can you show reverence and gratitude for the Spirit's work?

Day 23: 1 Peter 1:2 - "Who have been chosen according to the foreknowledge of God the Father, through the sanctifying work of the Spirit, to be obedient to Jesus Christ and sprinkled with his blood: Grace and peace be yours in abundance."

Question: How does the Spirit's sanctifying work lead you to obedience?

Day 24: 1 Peter 1:12 - "It was revealed to them that they were not serving themselves but you, when they spoke of the things that have now been told you by those who have preached the gospel to you by the Holy Spirit sent from heaven. Even angels long to look into these things."

Question: How can you serve others through the power of the Holy Spirit?

Day 25: 1 John 3:24 - "The one who keeps God's commands lives in him, and he in them. And this is how we know he lives in us: We know it by the Spirit he gave us."

Question: How does keeping God's commands connect you to the indwelling presence of the Holy Spirit?

Day 26: 1 John 4:13 - "This is how we know that we live in him and he in us: He has given us of his Spirit."

Question: How does the presence of the Holy Spirit assure you of your relationship with God?

Day 27: 1 John 5:6 - "This is the one who came by water and blood—Jesus Christ. He did not come by water only but by water and blood. And the Spirit testifies because the Spirit is the truth."

Question: How does the Spirit testify to the truth of Jesus Christ in your life? How have you experienced this witness in your heart?

Day 28: Revelation 2:7 - "Whoever has ears, let them hear what the Spirit says to the churches. To the victorious one, I will give the right to eat from the tree of life, which is in the paradise of God."

Question: Are you actively listening to what the Spirit is saying to you through the circumstances of your life, the words of others, and the Scriptures?

Day 29: Revelation 3:20 - "Here I am! I stand at the door and knock. If anyone hears my voice and opens the door, I will come in and eat with that person, and they will be with me."

Question: Is there any area of your life where you've closed the door on the Spirit's invitation? What would it look like to open that door today?

_____
_____
_____
_____
_____
_____
_____
_____
_____
_____
_____
_____
_____
_____
_____
_____
_____
_____
_____
_____
_____

Day 30: Revelation 22:17 - "The Spirit and the bride say, 'Come!' And let the one who hears say, 'Come!' Let the one who is thirsty come, and let the one who wishes take the gift of the water of life."

Question: How can you respond more to the Spirit's invitation to draw closer to God and experience His living water?

You Did It!!!!

Dear Reader,

Congratulations on completing the 30-Day Challenge! I celebrate with you as you reach this milestone in your journey of listening to the Holy Spirit.

Over the past month, you've intentionally created space to hear God's voice, to reflect on His Word, and to respond to His leading. You've taken significant steps toward cultivating a deeper relationship with the Holy Spirit and experiencing His empowering presence in your life.

This challenge has ignited your passion to continue seeking the Spirit's guidance in every area of your life. May you walk in the fullness of His power, experiencing the abundant life that Jesus promised and making a lasting impact on His Kingdom.

Well done, good and faithful servant!
With joy and blessings,
Your Sister in Christ

Appendices

Appendix A:
Scripture Meditation Guide

Grace:

Ephesians 2:8-9: "For it is by grace you have been saved, through faith—and this is not from yourselves, it is the gift of God— not by works, so that no one can boast."

2 Corinthians 12:9: "But he said to me, 'My grace is sufficient for you, for my power is made perfect in weakness.' Therefore I will boast all the more gladly about my weaknesses, so that Christ's power may rest on me."

Titus 2:11-12: "For the grace of God has appeared that offers salvation to all people. It teaches us to say 'No' to ungodliness and worldly passions, and to live self-controlled, upright and godly lives in this present age."

Compassion:

Matthew 9:36: "When he saw the crowds, he had compassion on them, because they were harassed and helpless, like sheep without a shepherd."

Colossians 3:12: "Therefore, as God's chosen people, holy and dearly loved, clothe yourselves with compassion, kindness, humility, gentleness and patience."

1 John 3:17: "If anyone has material possessions and sees a brother or sister in need but has no pity on them, how can the love of God be in that person?"

Forgiveness:

Ephesians 4:32: "Be kind and compassionate to one another, forgiving each other, just as in Christ God forgave you."

Matthew 6:14-15: "For if you forgive other people when they sin against you, your heavenly Father will also forgive you. But if you do not forgive others their sins, your Father will not forgive your sins."

Colossians 3:13: "Bear with each other and forgive one another if any of you has a grievance against someone. Forgive as the Lord forgave you."

Meditation Tips:

Choose a quiet space where you can focus without distractions.

Read the verse slowly and repeatedly, allowing the words to sink in.

Reflect on the meaning of the verse and how it applies to your life.

Pray and ask the Holy Spirit to illuminate the truth of the verse and help you apply it to your life.

Journal your thoughts and reflections, recording any insights or applications that come to mind.

Appendix B: Practical Exercises for Spirit Empowerment

1. Identifying Grievances:

- Take some time to reflect on your relationships. Is there anyone you need to forgive? Are you harboring any bitterness, anger, or resentment?

- Write down the names of those who have hurt you and the specific offenses.

- Pray for God's help in releasing these negative emotions and extending forgiveness.

2. Cultivating Gratitude:

- Keep a gratitude journal for one week. Each day, write down at least three things you are grateful for.

- Express your gratitude to God in prayer and to those around you.

- Notice how focusing on gratitude affects your attitude and outlook.

3. Practicing Kindness:

- Make a list of practical ways you can show kindness to others this week.
- Choose one act of kindness to perform each day.
- Reflect on how these acts of kindness impact both the giver and the receiver.

4. Developing Compassion:

- Choose a person in your life who is going through a difficult time.
- Practice active listening and seek to understand their perspective and emotions.
- Offer practical support and encouragement.
- Pray for them and ask God to give you His heart of compassion.

5. Surrendering to the Spirit:

- Set aside a specific time each day for prayer and reflection.
- Ask the Holy Spirit to reveal any areas of your life where you are holding back from His control.
- Surrender those areas to Him and ask for His strength to follow His leading.

Appendix C:
Daily Prayers for a Spirit-Filled Life

Morning Prayer:

"Holy Spirit, I invite You to fill me afresh today. Guide my thoughts, words, and actions. Empower me to live a life of grace, compassion, and forgiveness. Help me to be sensitive to Your promptings and obedient to Your leading. Use me as Your vessel to bring love and light to the world. Amen."

Midday Prayer:

"Lord Jesus, thank You for the gift of Your Holy Spirit. Help me to walk in Your Spirit today, moment by moment. Fill me with Your peace and joy. Empower me to love others as You have loved me. Amen."

Evening Prayer:

"Holy Spirit, I surrender this day to You. Thank You for Your presence and guidance. Forgive me for any way I have grieved You today. Fill me with Your love and peace as I rest. Amen."

This is just a starting point. Feel free to adapt these prayers and exercises to fit your own needs and preferences. The most important thing is to intentionally cultivate your relationship with the Holy Spirit and allow Him to empower you for a life of transformation.

Appendix D: Additional Resources

While the Bible remains the primary and ultimate source for understanding the Christian life and the work of the Holy Spirit, the following resources can provide further insights and practical guidance on the topics covered in this book:

On the Holy Spirit:

The Holy Spirit: Activating God's Power in Your Life by Charles Stanley explores the person and work of the Holy Spirit and offers practical guidance on how to experience His fullness and power in daily life.

The Pursuit of God by A.W. Tozer: This classic work delves into God's nature and our pursuit of intimacy with Him, emphasizing the vital role of the Holy Spirit in our spiritual journey.

Absolute Surrender by Andrew Murray challenges readers to fully surrender their lives to God, allowing the Holy Spirit to lead and transform them.

On Grace:

Amazing Grace by Charles Stanley: This book explores the depth and breadth of God's grace, revealing its transformative power in our lives.

The Grace of God by Andy Stanley examines the concept of grace in a contemporary context, challenging common misconceptions and highlighting its relevance for today's believers.

On Compassion:

Compassion: A Call to Counter Culture in a World of Inequality by Craig Groeschel: This book calls for a compassionate response to the suffering and injustice in the world and offers practical ways to make a difference.

The Power of Compassion by Joyce Meyer: This book explores the importance of compassion in our relationships and interactions, offering practical tips for cultivating a compassionate heart.

On Forgiveness:

Forgiveness: The Key to Inner Peace by Joyce Meyer: This book provides practical guidance on how to forgive others and experience the freedom and healing that forgiveness brings.

The Bait of Satan by John Bevere: This book exposes the destructive nature of unforgiveness and offers biblical principles for overcoming bitterness and resentment.

Remember: These resources are secondary to the Bible. Always prioritize studying the Scriptures and seeking the guidance of the

Holy Spirit as you seek to grow in understanding and applying these principles.

www.ingramcontent.com/pod-product-compliance
Lightning Source LLC
Chambersburg PA
CBHW070204100426
42743CB00013B/3047